REFLECTIONS ON GREECE

REFLECTIONS

WALKER AND COMPANY
NEW YORK

ON GREECE

PHOTOGRAPHS by
ROY MOORE

WITH QUOTATIONS from
NIKOS KAZANTZAKIS

First published in the United States of America in 1971 by the Walker Publishing Company, Inc.

Library of Congress Catalog Card Number: 73-166182

Designed by Carl Weiss

Printed in Japan

Published simultaneously in Canada by Fitzhenry & Whiteside, Limited, Toronto. ISBN: 0-8027-0362-3

Grateful acknowledgement is made to Simon & Schuster, Inc., Mrs. Helene N. Kazantzakis and Dr. Max Tau for permission to quote from *The Odyssey: A Modern Sequel, Report to Greco,* and *Journey to the Morea* by Nikos Kazantzakis and from *Nikos Kazantzakis: A Biography Based on His Letters* by Helene N. Kazantzakis.

꜓꜓꜓꜓꜓꜓꜓

THIS BOOK IS DEDICATED TO THE MEMORY OF

NIKOS KAZANTZAKIS,

AND TO THE FREEDOM-LOVING SPIRIT OF

THE GREEK PEOPLE,

EVERYWHERE.

꜓꜓꜓꜓꜓꜓꜓

ACKNOWLEDGEMENTS

I WISH TO THANK ALL OF THOSE who, through their numerous and varied kindnesses, have made this book possible. Preeminent among these have been Simon and Schuster, Inc., Dr. Max Tau, and Mrs. Helene Kazantzakis, all of whom have very kindly allowed me to quote from the works of the poet; Miss Helen D'Alessandro, my editor, whose patience and co-operation have surpassed all expectations; and my wife, Alma Moore, without whose insistence there would have been no book.

Especial thanks are due to the many Greek people, known and unknown to me, whose hospitality has made my visits to Greece among the more memorable moments of my life.

—ROY MOORE

GREECE

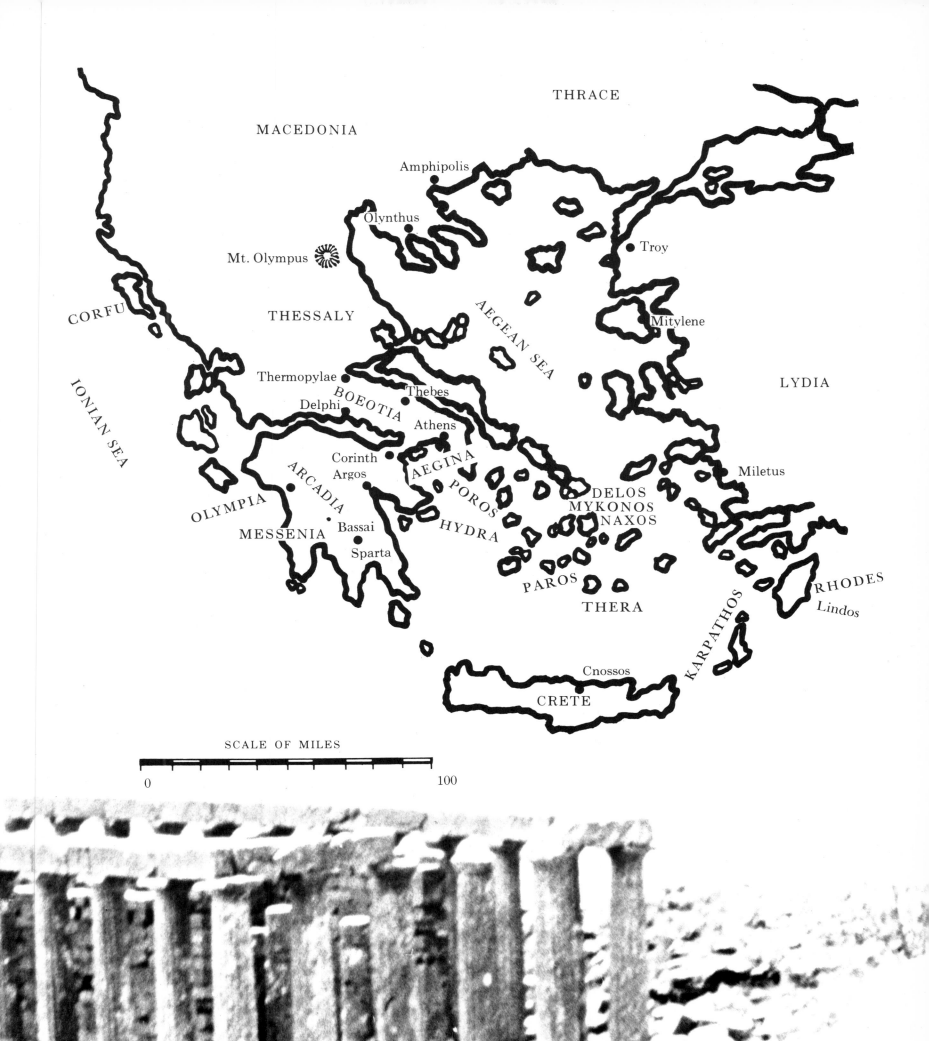

THRACE

MACEDONIA

Amphipolis

Olynthus

Mt. Olympus

Troy

CORFU

THESSALY

AEGEAN SEA

Mitylene

IONIAN SEA

Thermopylae

LYDIA

Delphi

BOEOTIA

Thebes

Athens

Corinth

Argos

AEGINA

Miletus

ARCADIA

OLYMPIA

POROS

DELOS

MESSENIA

Bassai

HYDRA

MYKONOS

NAXOS

Sparta

PAROS

THERA

RHODES

KARPATHOS

Lindos

Cnossos

CRETE

SCALE OF MILES

0   100

PREFACE

HOW A PEOPLE OF OBSCURE ORIGINS happened to settle in a country, little different from other Mediterranean lands, and then lay the foundations of nearly all that has come to be known as "Western" civilization will probably always remain an enigma. But it is hoped that this book will reflect some aspects of the physical, natural environment which may have fostered, perhaps demanded, the achievements which constitute the contributions of Greece and the Greeks to the history of mankind.

Artists of many lands have attempted to portray the essence of Greece, but, as C. Kerenyi, authority on the history of Greek life and religion, has said: ". . . the great painter, who could render . . . Greece . . . does not seem to have been born yet." Of the many writers and poets who have attempted to do so, of one who has come closest to capturing the "uniqueness" of Greece has been the Cretan poet, Nikos Kazantzakis. He has presented in a number of his many works a very deep and personal appraisal of the Greek landscape and the Greek spirit, the "spirit of place" which underlines the unique atmosphere of Greece—prompted by the same daimon which has prompted me to make the photographs included in this book, in an effort to express my personal reaction to Greece. For this reason, quotations from his works have been used throughout this volume. It is hoped that the combination of his imagery and the present collection of photographs might serve to arouse the interest and curiosity of the reader so that he, too, might go, look, and experience for himself the special quality or "ambiance" which makes Greece truly different.

On first viewing Greece, the immediate impression is one of terrific visual impact: the light, the color, the indescribable "rightness" of the scale and proportion. The physical scale of both landscape and architecture is acceptable—not overpowering, as in Rome or Egypt. Everything is on a scale whereby man may be impressed, even awed, but never overwhelmed. The landscape seems to adhere to this seemingly planned arrangement. There are mountains, even tall mountains—but never the Alps, nor the Rockies. There is ocean, more ocean than land—but never an Atlantic, nor a Pacific. The architecture, whether an ancient temple or a modern-day tenement, blends with, and becomes a part of the landscape, and vice versa; neither tending to overpower the other; complementary rather than competitive. To this living example of "measure," or what the Greeks call ʼαναλογια, has been added the typically Greek choice of site for their temples and monuments. Their location is always flawless. Even after centuries of earthquakes, landslides, and other manifestations of the ravages of time and nature, their choice of location cannot be faulted by the modern eye.

Another aspect of the Greek landscape which impresses and delights the viewer, especially if he is a photographer, is, of course, the light; and that light is indescribable. Its clarity, its purity, its seeming ability to illuminate and embellish all it touches, combined with completely uninhibited touches of color, by nature and by man, create an "ambiance" which is, in my experience, unequaled elsewhere.

This unique combination of landscape, architecture, and light, gentled by thousands of years of time and weather, has culminated in what Lord Kinross has so aptly described as "a country whose art is inseparable from its landscape and whose landscape is inseparable from its life . . . and Greece . . . is essentially, vividly, life."

"Greece," says Yannis Gaitanides, "lies before us, a complete firmly delineated world, a self-contained microcosm which includes every basic element of the earth, and all within range of our vision . . . each enhancing the other." And, as such, it is a masterpiece, unrivalled in visual excitement.

—— ROY MOORE

A BIOGRAPHICAL NOTE ON NIKOS KAZANTZAKIS

NIKOS KAZANTZAKIS, ACCLAIMED BY CRITICS AND SCHOLARS as one of the most versatile and eminent writers of our time, was born in Crete in 1883. Having spent his early years in his native island, he was graduated from the University of Athens in 1906, and later received a Doctor of Laws degree there. After studying literature and art in France, under the philosopher Henri Bergson, and in Germany and Italy, he returned to Greece. In 1919 he accepted a post as Director General of the Ministry of Public Welfare. In that capacity, he headed a mission that repatriated thousands of Greeks stranded in the Caucasus region through the vicissitudes of the First World War. His mission was credited with the safe return to Greece of some 150,000 persons.

Before the Second World War he lived on the island of Aegina, where he devoted himself to his philosophical and literary work. For a short while in 1945 he was Greek Minister of Education, and served as President of the Greek Society for Men of Letters. He also served, at that time, as Director of the Bureau of Translation of the Classics for the United Nations Educational Scientific and Cultural Organization.

With the idea of helping people of different nationalities to understand each other, Kazantzakis visited various European, Asian, and African countries, about which he wrote many travel books and articles in Greek. In 1945, he married Eleni Samios in Athens and lived with her on the French Riviera until his death in 1957.

Nominated several times for the Nobel Prize, Kazantzakis created numerous and varied works in the fields of philosophy, travel, drama, and poetry. His writings, including such masterworks as *Zorba the Greek, The Greek Passion,* and *Freedom or Death,* have appeared not only in Greek, but have been translated into English, German, and Swedish, as well as being adapted into the cinema of various languages. His crowning achievement, on which he worked over a period of twelve years, was *The Odyssey: a Modern Sequel,* a long epic poem on the fortunes of Odysseus, which begins where Homer's *Odyssey* ends. Published in the United States in 1958, in Kimon Friar's magnificent translation, it was acclaimed by critics and reviewers as one of the outstanding literary events of our time.

┏┛┗┛┗┛┗┛┗┛┗┛┗┛┗┛┗┓

. . . high time for myths and legends to walk the earth once more . . .

THE ODYSSEY: A MODERN SEQUEL

. . . stay wide awake . . . beware of spells
. . . we're entering magic . . .

THE ODYSSEY: A MODERN SEQUEL

BASSAI: TEMPLE OF APOLLO
EPIKOURIOS (READY TO SUCCOR).

. . . an austere mountain, fragrant with
savory and thyme . . . utterly forsaken.   REPORT TO GRECO

BASSAI: MT. KOTILION . . . IN AWE-INSPIRING SOLITUDE,
AT THE TOP OF THE RIDGE.

. . . the lone mountain tree is beaten by all winds . . .

THE ODYSSEY: A MODERN SEQUEL

BASSAI: CONSTRUCTED 420–417 B.C. BY THE PHYGALIANS, IN GRATITUDE TO APOLLO, WHO HAD SAVED THEM FROM A PLAGUE.

. . . suddenly, the heart of the Pelopones-
sus . . . the famous temple of Apollo at
Bassai.

REPORT TO GRECO

BASSAI: THE MOST ADMIRED
TEMPLE IN THE PELOPONNESUS,
CONTAINING THE OLDEST
KNOWN SPECIMEN OF CORIN-
THIAN COLUMN. FRIEZE AND
METOPES ARE NOW IN THE
BRITISH MUSEUM.

. . . now earth shall bloom once more,
and the stones sprout with grass.

THE ODYSSEY: A MODERN SEQUEL

OLYMPIA: SACRED TO THE
GODS WERE THE ROSE, THE
MYRTLE, AND THE POPPY.

. . . the . . . sea . . . opened her frothing
mouth and crunched the . . . shore . . .

THE ODYSSEY: A MODERN SEQUEL

PAROS: PEBBLES ON SHORE,
LIKE MOST OF THE ISLAND, ARE
OF PARIAN MARBLE, VALUED
HIGHLY BY SCULPTORS OF CLAS-
SICAL GREECE. QUARRIES ON MT.
MARPESSA ARE STILL WORKED
FOR LOCAL USE.

. . . rowboats . . . with oars crossed on their chests, slept calmly by the white shore's foam.

THE ODYSSEY: A MODERN SEQUEL

MYKONOS: TYPICALLY BRIGHTLY PAINTED BOAT WITH DRIED NETS READY FOR THE EVENING'S FISHING.

. . . all doors are traps which we fling open with our dreams . . .

THE ODYSSEY: A MODERN SEQUEL

LINDOS: DOORWAY REFLECT-
ING VARIED INFLUENCES OF
GREEK, CRUSADER, AND TURK-
ISH ARCHITECTURE, FOUND
THROUGHOUT RHODES. PEB-
BLED-MOSAIC DOORSTEPS ARE
ALSO COMMON IN THIS AREA.

. . . in haze a ghostly city . . . in the sun's
silent beams . . .

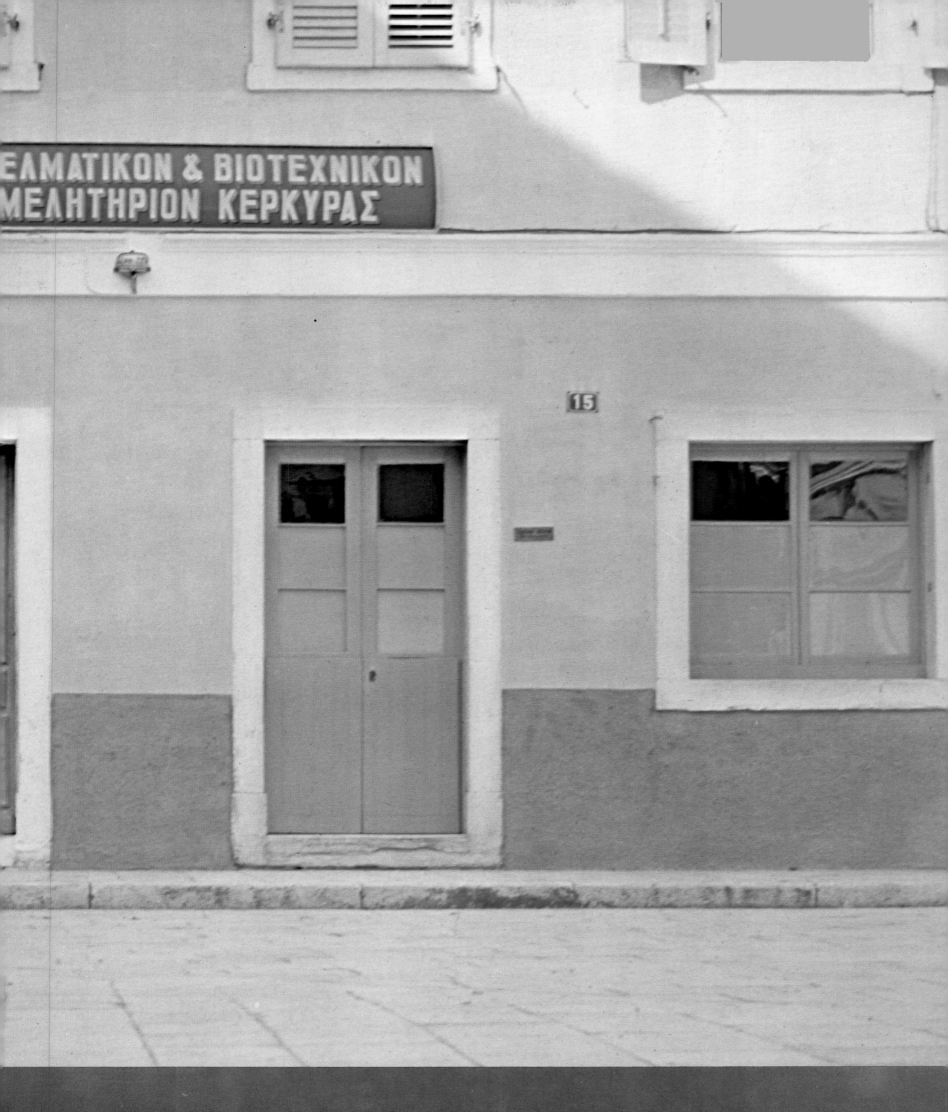

CORFU: DESERTED SQUARE IN THE CENTER OF CORFU
TOWN. THIS AREA IS USUALLY ALIVE WITH PEOPLE, BUT IT'S
SIESTA TIME.

. . . and I felt as only one thing exists: the light . . .

NIKOS KAZANTZAKIS: A BIOGRAPHY
BASED ON HIS LETTERS

MYKONOS: CHURCH OF PA-
RAPORTIANI, ONE OF MORE
THAN 350 CHURCHES AND CHAP-
ELS ON THIS TINY ISLAND.

Time . . . with swift sleight-of-hand.
grasps shadows, light and air, then shapes
. . . the wonders of the world . . .

THE ODYSSEY: A MODERN SEQUEL

DELPHI: TEMPLE OF APOLLO,
ERECTED CIRCA 505 B.C., BE-
FORE THE PHAEDRIADES ROCKS,
A PART OF MT. PARNASSUS, HOME
OF THE MUSES.

. . . leaves flashed, the fragrant plants filled all ·the air with scent . . . the sun sailed through the mists and the stones smiled . . .

THE ODYSSEY: A MODERN SEQUEL

DELPHI: POOL IN GYMNA-SIUM, WHERE ATHLETES PAR-TICIPATING IN THE PYTHIAN GAMES BATHED BEFORE THE COMPETITION, PURIFYING THEMSELVES FOR THE CON-TEST.

. . . stone seats, worn smooth by time . . .

THE ODYSSEY: A MODERN SEQUEL

DELPHI: STADIUM, SITE OF
THE PYTHIAN GAMES, CON-
STRUCTED OF PARNASSIAN LIME-
STONE FROM THE SURROUND-
ING MOUNTAIN.

. . . a temple perched on some high
rock . . .

THE ODYSSEY: A MODERN SEQUEL

DELPHI: THOLOS, IN THE
MARMARIA. A MARBLE RO-
TUNDA, ONE OF THE MOST ELE-
GANT PIECES OF ARCHITECTURE
OF THE 4TH CENTURY (370–360)
B.C., WHOSE EXACT USE AND
PURPOSE ARE STILL UNKNOWN.

. . . stood straight like mighty pillars and
supported God.

THE ODYSSEY: A MODERN SEQUEL

DELPHI: TEMPLE OF APOLLO.

Day climbed, and thistles on the sharp
crags bloomed with light . . .

THE ODYSSEY: A MODERN SEQUEL

CORFU: ANOTHER EXAMPLE
OF THE PERSISTENCE OF VEGE-
TATION OF ALL KINDS, DESPITE
THE HARSH ENVIRONMENT.

. . . around each corner inexpressibly delightful discoveries; white, white stair-cases . . .

NIKOS KAZANTZAKIS: A BIOGRAPHY
BASED ON HIS LETTERS

MYKONOS: IT SEEMS THAT NEARLY EVERYTHING ON THIS GREEK ISLAND IS WHITEWASHED —BUILDINGS, STAIRWAYS, EVEN THE STREETS!

. . . an azure window opens toward the
sky . . .

REPORT TO GRECO

HYDRA: TONES AND TEX-
TURES BECOME PAINTINGS IN
THE GREEK LIGHT.

Whoever sets foot on this island senses
his soul begin to grow.

REPORT TO GRECO

CRETE: IN A LAND WHERE
ARABLE LAND IS LIMITED, THE
HILLS AND MOUNTAINS ARE
TERRACED AND CULTIVATED AS
HIGH AS ANYTHING EDIBLE
WILL GROW.

. . . islands sprang up . . . glowed and
swayed . . . above the waves . . .

THE ODYSSEY: A MODERN SEQUEL

CORFU: PONDIKINISI BAY, OFF
CORFU.

... the rock, the bare dry rock I've loved
and longed for ...

THE ODYSSEY: A MODERN SEQUEL

THERA: IN THE VOLCANIC
SOIL OF SANTORINI (THERA'S
OTHER NAME—IN HONOR OF
SAINT IRENE) WILDFLOWERS
PERSIST IN BLOSSOMING.

. . . the foaming waters to the sky's far
rim reddened like coppery wine.

. . . doors gape open . . . wild grasses . . .
overrun the walls . . .

JOURNEY TO THE MOREA

HYDRA: THOUGH DESERTED
AND UNKEMPT, THE DOORWAYS
STILL EXERCISE THEIR FASCINA-
TION.

. . . hungry vines . . . climbed through the jagged ruins and browsed on broken stones . . .

THE ODYSSEY: A MODERN SEQUEL

OLYMPIA: WILDFLOW-
ERS AND VINES COMPLEMENT
THE RUINS.

. . . flowers . . . turned toward the sun
and trailed its light till . . . darkness . . .

THE ODYSSEY: A MODERN SEQUEL

OLYMPIA: THE GODS MAY
HAVE DEPARTED, BUT NATURE
STILL MAKES ITS VOTIVE OFFER-
INGS.

. . . boughs of the almond . . . in Spring's giddy swell . . . cast flowers . . .

THE ODYSSEY: A MODERN SEQUEL

OLYMPIA: TEMPLE OF HERA, ONE OF THE OLDEST TEMPLES KNOWN (7TH CENTURY B.C.). IN THE CELLA STOOD THE FAMOUS STATUE OF HERMES BY PRAXY-TILES, NOW IN THE MUSEUM AT OLYMPIA.

. . . Spring had come in the warm night
and filled their fields with flowers . . .

THE ODYSSEY: A MODERN SEQUEL

OLYMPIA: DAISIES SHEL-
TERED BY A TIPPED OLYMPIAN
COLUMN.

I walked back and forth among the ruins
. . . joyfully viewing the shell-bearing
stones employed to build the temples.

NIKOS KAZANTZAKIS: A BIOGRAPHY
BASED ON HIS LETTERS

OLYMPIA: TEMPLE OF ZEUS,
WHICH ONCE CONTAINED THE
CHRYSELEPHANTINE STATUE OF
THE FATHER OF THE GODS BY
PHIDEAS. ONE OF THE SEVEN
"WONDERS" OF THE ANCIENT
WORLD, IT WAS CARRIED OFF TO
CONSTANTINOPLE IN 475 A.D.
AND DISAPPEARED. THE CON-
CHIFEROUS STONE USED IN THE
CONSTRUCTION OF THE TEMPLE
CAME FROM THE NEIGHBORING
QUARRIES AT SARAKI.

. . . when earth had filled with flowers
and fields with grass . . .

OLYMPIA: WILDFLOW-
ERS AND FALLEN CORINTHIAN
CAPITOLS ARE SCATTERED
AMONG FRAGMENTS OF THE
TEMPLE OF ZEUS.

. . . the marble lions gaped and laughed . . .

THE ODYSSEY: A MODERN SEQUEL

OLYMPIA: STOREYARD OUT-
SIDE OF THE MUSEUM, WHERE
EXCAVATED FRAGMENTS AWAIT
EXAMINATION AND CLASSIFICA-
TION. DARK STONE OBJECTS
IN BACKGROUND ARE WEIGHTS,
CARRIED BY BROAD-JUMPERS IN
THE OLYMPIC GAMES TO IN-
CREASE THE LENGTH OF THEIR
JUMPS.

. . . clusters of wisteria, undulating ser-
pents, perpendicular waterfalls, moving
images . . .

NIKOS KAZANTZAKIS: A BIOGRAPHY
BASED ON HIS LETTERS

AEGINA: HOUSE DAMAGED
BY EARTHQUAKE AND BEAUTI-
FIED BY CLIMBING WISTERIA.

. . . the sun, like a night lamp, transforming the sea into an iridescent cloth of mother-of-pearl . . .

NIKOS KAZANTZAKIS: A BIOGRAPHY
BASED ON HIS LETTERS

ATTICA: VIEW OF THE BAY
AT SOUNION.

. . . all doors adorned with different knockers . . . but the mind . . . opens and walks through.

THE ODYSSEY: A MODERN SEQUEL

MYKONOS: ANOTHER BEAU-
TIFULLY TINTED DOOR IN
A GLEAMING WHITEWASHED
WALL.

. . . and heaving clouds tossed like frenetic dragons in the lowering sky . . .

THE ODYSSEY: A MODERN SEQUEL

PAROS: ONE OF THE SUDDEN STORMS WHICH SPRING UP IN THIS AREA, DRIVING THE FISHERMEN INTO THE NEAREST PORT AND TRANSFORMING THE USUALLY PLACID MEDITERRANEAN INTO A WATERY MAELSTORM. FORTUNATELY, THEY PASS ALMOST AS QUICKLY AS THEY APPEAR.

. . . in the sun's blaze . . . the sea licked
the seashore with her rasping tongue . . .

THE ODYSSEY: A MODERN SEQUEL

PAROS: SMALL BAY ON THE
ROCKY COAST . . . NEAR PAROS
TOWN.

. . . its flat, whitewashed roofs, sparkling
like a city on the moon, over a dark blue
and green sea.

NIKOS KAZANTZAKIS: A BIOGRAPHY
BASED ON HIS LETTERS

MYKONOS: DUE TO THE
VERY SLIGHT TIDE IN THIS
PART OF THE MEDITERRANEAN,
HOUSES ARE BUILT AND INHAB-
ITED RIGHT AT THE WATER-
LINE. TOURISTS SOMETIMES
CALL THIS AREA "LITTLE
VENICE."

On the white pebbled shore, the town
burst like a rose . . .

THE ODYSSEY: A MODERN SEQUEL

MYKONOS: THE WINDWARD SIDE OF THE ISLAND.

. . . on a far isle I saw a windmill creak
its   wings . . . in   windless   calm . . . no
grain to grind . . .

THE ODYSSEY: A MODERN SEQUEL

MYKONOS: ALTHOUGH
SOME OF THE WINDMILLS ARE
STILL OPERABLE, TODAY THEY
ARE MAINTAINED MOSTLY FOR
THE BENEFIT OF THE TOURIST.
AT ONE TIME, GRAIN WAS SHIP-
PED FROM ISLANDS ALL OVER
THE AREA FOR GRINDING, BUT
TODAY IT IS NO LONGER ECO-
NOMICALLY FEASIBLE.

. . . the sun beat down the . . . sandy
reach of shore . . .

THE ODYSSEY: A MODERN SEQUEL

MYKONOS: TYPICAL EX-
AMPLE OF THE FISHERMEN'S
CHAPELS, FREQUENTLY BUILT
TO HONOR WHATEVER SAINT
HAD SAVED THE FISHERMAN
FROM PERIL AT SEA. PRACTI-
CALLY, IT IS A GOOD AREA IN
WHICH THE FISHERMAN CAN
SPREAD HIS NETS TO DRY
IN A SANCTIFIED ATMOSPHERE
WHICH JUST MIGHT INSURE A
GOOD CATCH ON THE NEXT
TRIP.

...sentries keeping guard in chiseled stone ...

THE ODYSSEY: A MODERN SEQUEL

DELOS: REMNANTS OF THE TERRACE OF LIONS, GUARDIANS OF THE AREA SACRED TO APOLLO, PRESENTED TO THE SANCTUARY BY THE INHABITANTS OF THE ISLAND OF NAXOS.

The whole of the charming temple lives
and breathes . . .

REPORT TO GRECO

DELOS: IN THE AREA DED-
ICATED TO "FOREIGN GODS,"
THE TEMPLE OF ISIS, THE MOST
WIDELY WORSHIPED EGYPTIAN
GODDESS IN GREECE.

. . . on the sea's rim, like a dawn's glow-
ing cloud, the sun-washed, rock-strewn
body of my longed-for land . . .

THE ODYSSEY: A MODERN SEQUEL

CORFU: TYPICAL ROCKY
COAST OF THE LUSH, WELL-
WATERED IONIAN ISLAND.

... I shall taste the world in flower ...

THE ODYSSEY: A MODERN SEQUEL

OLYMPIA: LIKE ATHENA,
WILDFLOWERS SPRING FROM
THE TEMPLE OF ZEUS.

. . . deserted . . . besieged and . . . overrun by fragrant greens . . .

JOURNEY TO THE MOREA

AEGEAN ISLAND: WEATH-
ERED DOORWAY CONTRASTS
WITH THE STARK WHITE WALLS.

...life...entwines among the ruins, deep-rooted like ivy...

JOURNEY TO THE MOREA

MYKONOS: CHAPEL AND RE-
MAINS OF ONE WHICH WAS DE-
STROYED BY EARTHQUAKE.

... silence ... with its two stone lion
guards ...

THE ODYSSEY: A MODERN SEQUEL

RHODES: COURTYARD EN-
HANCED WITH ARCHEOLOGICAL
DISCOVERIES, AND TWO MEM-
BERS OF A TRIBE PLENTIFUL ON
THIS ISLAND.

. . . like bird tracks on soft clay, the . . .
inscriptions squirmed, a swarm of ants
. . . telling of ancient tales and gallant
deeds . . .

THE ODYSSEY: A MODERN SEQUEL

RHODES: INSCRIBED STONE
ON THE ACROPOLIS AT LINDOS.

. . . not a soul in sight, doors shut . . .

REPORT TO GRECO

AEGEAN ISLAND: A CLOSED
DOOR, A SHUTTERED WINDOW,
SOLITUDE . . .

. . . full of light . . . the mountains serene
. . . the earth covered with greenery.

NIKOS KAZANTZAKIS: A BIOGRAPHY
BASED ON HIS LETTERS

CRETE: CRETAN LANDSCAPE, WILD, ROCKY, AUSTERE, BUT GREEN AND CULTIVATED.
THE TREES ARE PERMANENTLY BENT IN THE DIRECTION OF THE PREVAILING WINDS.

. . . flowers spring from flame-hot stones . . .

REPORT TO GRECO

PELOPONNESUS: THE VEGE-
TATION SEEMS TO EXIST ON SUN
AND AIR ALONE.

. . . all opposites join together, mix, and are reconciled here, creating the supreme miracle, harmony.

REPORT TO GRECO

LINDOS: CENTRAL STAIR-CASE AND VAST DOUBLE-WINGED PORTICO; APPROACH TO THE SANCTUARY OF ATHENA LINDIA AT LINDOS.

The meadow was strewn with poppies, big yellow daisies . . . sweetly scenting the coast.

NIKOS KAZANTZAKIS: A BIOGRAPHY
BASED ON HIS LETTERS

RHODES: FIELDS OF WILD-
FLOWERS APPEAR EACH SPRING
BEFORE THE ACROPOLIS AT
LINDOS.

... like spinning foam on the ... wandering wave ...

THE ODYSSEY: A MODERN SEQUEL

RHODES: LOOKING FROM THE HEIGHTS OF THE ACROPOLIS AT LINDOS, DOWN TO THE SEA. ST. PAUL IS SUPPOSED TO HAVE LANDED HERE, AFTER BEING SHIPWRECKED.

...the ... doorway of a large, half-crumbling house.

REPORT TO GRECO

AEGINA: WOOD AND STONE,
TEMPERED BY TIME.

. . . his vessel lightly tossed upon the sun-
washed waters . . .

THE ODYSSEY: A MODERN SEQUEL

MYKONOS: THE NETS, THESE
DAYS, ARE MADE OF NYLON!

When noontime dripped on earth and
shadows huddled close . . .

THE ODYSSEY: A MODERN SEQUEL

THERA (SANTORINI): A
SHUTTERED WINDOW, A SCAL-
LOPPED SHADOW, A STILL LIFE
ON A WHITEWASHED WALL.

The . . . gate was opened, the courtyards
deserted . . .

REPORT TO GRECO

LINDOS: MOSAIC PAVEMENT,
HAND-LAID IN BLACK AND WHITE
PEBBLES, TYPICAL OF MANY
RHODIAN COURTYARDS.

. . . a   butterfly. . . its . . . downy   wings prismatic . . .

THE ODYSSEY: A MODERN SEQUEL

. . . the town spread gleaming white between two mountain slopes . . .

CRETE: RUINS OF PREHIS-
TORIC, NEOLITHIC TOWN OF
GOURNIA.

...and from the ... casements, gardens
slowly strolled.

THE ODYSSEY: A MODERN SEQUEL

CORFU: VIEW FROM WINDOW
OF MUSEUM IN CORFU TOWN.

The small island turned to mist . . . and
slowly faded from the mind . . .

THE ODYSSEY: A MODERN SEQUEL

CORFU: THE MONASTERY
VALACHERNES AT THE HEAD OF
ITS NARROW BREAKWATER, IN
PONDIKINISI BAY.

. . . arcades . . . squares . . . the whole city a miracle . . .

NIKOS KAZANTZAKIS: A BIOGRAPHY
BASED ON HIS LETTERS

CORFU: REMINDER OF FRENCH OCCUPATION OF CORFU;
LOCAL REPRODUCTION OF PARIS'S RUE DE RIVOLI.

The church . . . shines gently with its . . .
lean graceful belltower.

JOURNEY TO THE MOREA

CORFU: CHURCH, ACROSS
CRICKET FIELD; REMINDER,
ALONG WITH GINGER BEER, OF
THE ENGLISH OCCUPATION OF
CORFU.

. . . azure seashores gleamed and glowed as gentle light dripped softly on old olive trees and all the bare and billowing mountains smelled of thyme.

THE ODYSSEY: A MODERN SEQUEL

CORFU: BAY ON WEST COAST OF CORFU. ONE OF THE LOVE-LIEST SPOTS IN THE ISLAND.

A magic portal opened . . . and conducted me into an astonishing world.

REPORT TO GRECO

THERA (SANTORINI):
STREET IN TOWN CONSTRUCTED
ON THE RIDGE OF A VOLCANIC
CRATER.

In their fragmented dance, the austere
columns . . . bear witness to the . . .
ravage . . .

NIKOS KAZANTZAKIS: A BIOGRAPHY
BASED ON HIS LETTERS

AEGINA: TEMPLE OF APHAIA,
FAMOUS FOR ITS SITUATION, ITS
STATE OF PRESERVATION, AND
ITS SCULPTURES (NOW IN MU-
NICH). ARCHITECTURALLY, THE
MOST PERFECTLY DEVELOPED OF
THE LATE ARCHAIC TEMPLES IN
GREECE.

. . . hangs in the blue air . . . nibbled by the four winds . . .

THE ODYSSEY: A MODERN SEQUEL

CRETE: SHRINE OF ST. GEORGE, PERCHED ON SIDE OF MOUNTAIN, ON ROAD BETWEEN HERAKLION AND AGIOS NIKOLAOS.

. . . we eat oranges . . . and stand . . . star-
ing . . .

NIKOS KAZANTZAKIS: A BIOGRAPHY
BASED ON HIS LETTERS

LINDOS: STILL LIFE ON THE
ACROPOLIS OF LINDOS.

. . . so doors were shut . . . and friends
sat down to feast . . .

THE ODYSSEY: A MODERN SEQUEL

AEGINA: PAINT-BOX, CON-
VERTED FROM OLD WOODEN
DOORSTEP, USED BY ITINERANT
PAINTER OF DOORS AND WIN-
DOWS. IN THIS PHOTOGRAPH,
HE'S INSIDE, HAVING LUNCH
WITH ONE OF HIS CLIENTS.

. . . casements and doors glowed suddenly . . .

THE ODYSSEY: A MODERN SEQUEL

AEGINA: FINISHED WORK OF
DOOR-PAINTER.

...when...you come at dawn or dusk
to stroll amid our narrow lanes...

THE ODYSSEY: A MODERN SEQUEL

AEGINA: STREET SCENE IN
AEGINA.

. . . I gazed between the golden columns
. . . that . . . laughed in blazing sun . . .

THE ODYSSEY: A MODERN SEQUEL

ATHENS: COLUMNS OF THE HE-
PHAESTON (THESEUM) AT SUN-
SET. NATURE PAINTS A DOOR-
WAY!

If we should ever shape our gods, we'll take for measure our own proud spirit at its passion's highest peak!

THE ODYSSEY: A MODERN SEQUEL

ATHENS: TEMPLE OF HE-
PHAESTOS (INCORRECTLY AT-
TRIBUTED, FOR MANY YEARS, TO
THESEUS). APPROPRIATED AS
CHRISTIAN CHURCH IN THE 5TH
CENTURY A.D., AND, THEREBY,
BETTER PRESERVED THAN MOST.
IT IS OLDER THAN THE PARTHE-
NON, AND THE MOST INTACT OF
ALL GREEK TEMPLES, TODAY.

. . . chiseled in stone . . . gigantic gods
loomed high and shone . . .
THE ODYSSEY: A MODERN SEQUEL

ATHENS: THE AGORA AND
THE TEMPLE OF HEPHAESTOS.

... softly melting in the sun's fierce blaze ... struck deep roots in the rock clefts ...

THE ODYSSEY: A MODERN SEQUEL

OLYMPIA: THE INNOCENT
RED POPPY BRIGHTENS MUCH
OF THE GREEK LANDSCAPE.

. . . all streets spread wide in welcome . . .

THE ODYSSEY: A MODERN SEQUEL

MYKONOS: AEGEAN AC-
CENTS OF COLOR.

. . . we build boats, splice ropes, calk seams, patch up our tattered sails, study the weather, then set sail . . .

THE ODYSSEY: A MODERN SEQUEL

MYKONOS: FISHERMEN'S COVE.

. . . bronzed fishermen . . . their nets . . .
gleaming in sun . . .

THE ODYSSEY: A MODERN SEQUEL

MYKONOS: THE COLORS OF
THE NETS ARE TYPICALLY GREEK!

. . . the town . . . shone in rose-rays of the
setting sun.

THE ODYSSEY: A MODERN SEQUEL

AEGINA: STREET IN AEGINA.

. . . streets and lanes with all their trib-
utaries rolled like streams . . .

THE ODYSSEY: A MODERN SEQUEL

THERA (SANTORINI):
STREET SCENE IN TONES OF
BROWN.

. . . heaped upon the piers from the long-voyaged, many-oared . . . foreign ships.

THE ODYSSEY: A MODERN SEQUEL

MYKONOS: TYPICAL BIT OF
INTER-ISLAND FREIGHT, FOUND
ON DOCK AT MYKONOS.

. . . a ripe and downy dandelion . . . scattered . . . seeds . . . along the morning air.

THE ODYSSEY: A MODERN SEQUEL

ATHENS: UNDOUBTEDLY,
THE LARGEST DANDELION I HAVE
EVER ENCOUNTERED, GROWING
ON THE HILL OF PHILOPAPPOS.

The mountain summits swooned in pal-
lid dusk . . .

THE ODYSSEY: A MODERN SEQUEL

ATHENS: SUNSET OVER THE
HILL OF PHILOPAPPOS.

. . . a carved stone that greets the sun
each dawn . . .

THE ODYSSEY: A MODERN SEQUEL

OLYMPIA: CORINTHIAN DE-
TAIL.

. . . narrow little streets . . . wash hang-
ing on the balconies . . .

NIKOS KAZANTZAKIS: A BIOGRAPHY
BASED ON HIS LETTERS

NAUPLION: STREET SCENE.

. . . through . . . open doors . . . dreams like peacocks stroll . . .

THE ODYSSEY: A MODERN SEQUEL

MYKONOS: A WHITEWASHED STREET, A PAINTED DOOR, A WELCOME GUEST.

. . . raise like a column all our hopes . . .

THE ODYSSEY: A MODERN SEQUEL

ATHENS: TEMPLE OF OLYM-
PIAN ZEUS, BEGUN IN 6TH CEN-
TURY B.C. BY PEISISTRATOS; NOT
COMPLETED UNTIL A.D. 131–132
BY THE ROMAN EMPEROR HA-
DRIAN.

. . . tall grasses rose from the cracked skulls of princes . . .

THE ODYSSEY: A MODERN SEQUEL

OLYMPIA: WILDFLOW-
ERS OVERRUN THE RUINS.

. . . a faultless thought enmarbled . . .
austere, sublime, perfect.

ATHENS: PARTHENON.

. . . life has no higher peak, no greater
bloom . . .

THE ODYSSEY: A MODERN SEQUEL

ATHENS: PARTHENON.

... a sun-shot stately column ...

THE ODYSSEY: A MODERN SEQUEL

ATHENS: PARTHENON.

... gleaming rocks that laugh when struck by sun, after rain ...

THE ODYSSEY: A MODERN SEQUEL

ATHENS: PARTHENON.

. . . young girls . . . their water pitchers
high on upright heads . . .

THE ODYSSEY: A MODERN SEQUEL

ATHENS: PORCH OF THE
CARIATIDES, THE ERECTHEUM,
ON THE ACROPOLIS.

...leaves slowly danced and bid the
light farewell...

THE ODYSSEY: A MODERN SEQUEL

ATHENS: SUNSET, FROM THE
HILL OF THE MUSES.

Space . . . conquered . . . infinity entered this . . . magical parallelogram . . . and took its repose there.

ATHENS: PARTHENON.

... on mountain slopes night stepped
with crimson feet ...

THE ODYSSEY: A MODERN SEQUEL

ATHENS: HILL OF THE
NYMPHS, WITH ASTRONOMICAL
OBSERVATORY, AT SUNSET,
FROM THE ACROPOLIS.

HISTORICAL NOTES ON THE TEMPLE SITES

OLYMPIA

꒫꒩꒫꒩꒫꒩꒫꒩꒫꒩꒫꒩꒫꒩꒫

IN THE COMPARATIVELY ISOLATED WESTERN PELOPONNESUS, removed from the most popular routes of invading enemies, in an area well watered and fertile, stands the valley of Olympia. In its geographic and political seclusion on the edge of the Alpheus River, Olympia, in ancient times, was venerated as a religious and athletic center—the athletics, the Olympic Games, having existed into modern times. Originally sacred and inviolable, the month of the Olympic Games was observed by all of Greece, all hostilities were suspended, and all who could flocked to the site at Olympia for religious worship and attendance at the games. Gradually the site was enriched by magnificent buildings and works of art, which were gifts and thank-offerings from the winners and their supporters, and was visited by thousands of Greeks and foreigners on every fourth year.

Among the most magnificent attractions at Olympia was the temple of Zeus, built 468–456 B.C. by the architect Libon of Ellis with the proceeds from the spoils taken by the Ellians from the Pisans in 468 B.C. Situated within the Altis, or sacred enclosure, the temple was in the Doric style, built of conglomerate stone and coated with painted stucco. It housed one of the "wonders" of the ancient world, the famous chryselephantine statue of Zeus by Phideas. In A.D. 475 the statue was removed from the temple and carried off to Constantinople, where it disappeared, presumably destroyed by fire. In A.D. 426 Theodosius II ordered all pagan temples destroyed, and the great temple of Zeus did not escape. An earthquake in the 6th century A.D. destroyed all that remained.

Also within the Altis stood one of the oldest Greek temples known, the Heraion. Dedicated in the 6th century B.C. to Hera, the wife of Zeus, it was built over the remains of two earlier temples. Successive restorations have resulted in a number of architectural anomalies. The large roof-tiles which once covered the temple are in the Museum. Housed in this temple was the world-famous statue of Hermes by Praxiteles, which can now be seen in the Olympia Museum, the only surviving example of this great sculptor's work.

Outside the Altis is found a workshop-studio where Phideas is supposed to have fashioned his colossal statue of Zeus, then transported it, piece by piece, to its site in the temple.

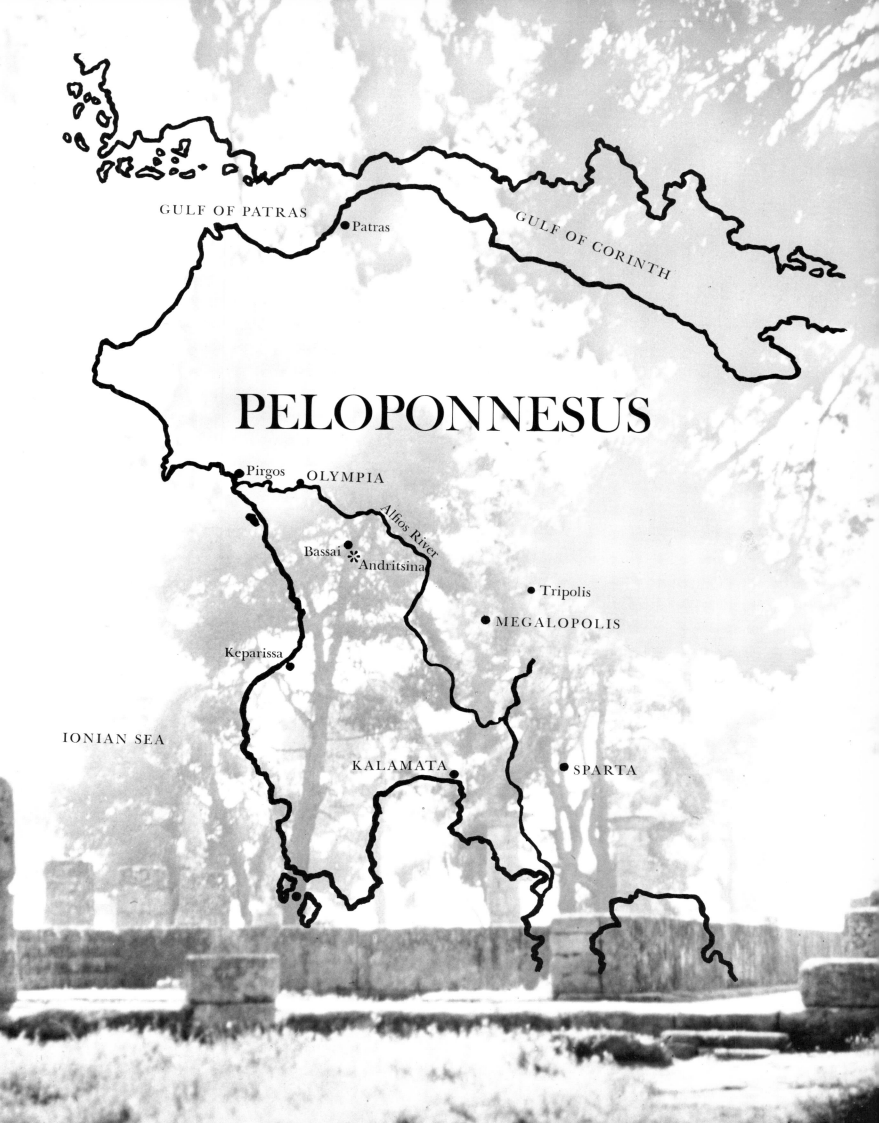

GULF OF PATRAS

GULF OF CORINTH

• Patras

PELOPONNESUS

• Pirgos OLYMPIA

Alfios River

Bassai ✳ Andritsina

• Tripolis

● MEGALOPOLIS

Keparissa

IONIAN SEA

KALAMATA

● SPARTA

BASSAI– TEMPLE OF APOLLO

IN ARCADIA, IN THE WESTERN PELOPONNESUS, 3900 feet above sea level, the Temple of Apollo Epikouros stands on a narrow platform on Mt. Kotylos. Built around 450 B.C. by the Phygalians out of gratitude to Apollo for having saved them from a plague, the structure of gray-blue limestone with veining of lilac and rose offers a fascinating contrast between the work of man and the surrounding wild and unspoiled work of nature. In an effort to outrival the recently completed colossal temple of Zeus at Olympia, the Phygalians secured the services of the architect Ictinus, who later constructed the Parthenon in Athens. Here, amid the rugged grandeur at Bassai (the ravines), Ictinus designed what is now the second-best preserved temple in Greece. He did not employ on this earlier temple the curved lines and tilting columns which make the Parthenon optically perfect, but the results of his design, in the case of Bassai, was a masterpiece of grace, elegance and refinement.

Of local limestone, the temple possesses several anomalies which are unusual for a classic Greek temple of the Dorian order. It was, for one thing, aligned from north to south, rather than the usual east-west orientation. Whether this was due to the pecularities of the site, or whether there was some other reason, is unknown. The temple contained a single column, at the rear of the cella, with a Corinthian capital. This is the first known use of such a column in a Greek temple. There was also a unique interior frieze, depicting battles between the Greeks and the Amazons, and a battle between the Centaurs, legendary half-man, half-horse creatures, and the Lapiths.

The isolated position of the temple prevented looting and quarrying which has destroyed so many of the Greek monuments, and in 1764, when it was discovered by the French architect Bocher, it had been virtually unvisited and untouched since pagan times—forgotten by man for over two thousand years. At the time of the discovery, although some of the temple and much of the sculpture had fallen to earth as a result of earthquake and storm, most of the material was found and eventually replaced. On his second visit to the temple site, Bocher was captured and murdered by local brigands, who were more interested in the money he was carrying (with which he had planned to hire excavators) than in the reconstruction of Apollo's shrine.

In 1812, Cockerell and Foster made a bid to the Turkish occupiers of Greece to buy the interior frieze and some of the sculpture. This offer having been refused, the frieze was secretly removed by sixty men who had come by boat in the middle of the night from the island of Zante. In 1816 the frieze was purchased by the Prince Regent of England and today it can be seen in the British Museum, along with the "original" Caryatid from the Erectheum on the Acropolis in Athens.

DELPHI

CLINGING TO A SPUR OF MT. PARNASSUS, home of the Muses, towering over the Pleistos Valley, which contains the immense olive grove, property of the god, Delphi occupies one of the most beautiful, awe-inspiring sites in all of Greece. When the cult of Phoebus Apollo, known to the Cretans as Apollo Delphinius and worshiped by them in the shape of a dolphin, arrived at Delphi, it had long been a site of the worship of the earth-goddess, Gea, and had already achieved fame as the home of the serpent Pytho and its oracle, the Pythoness. Defeating the serpent, legend tells us, Apollo and his followers took over the shrine and the prophetess. By the time of the formation of the Amphictyonic Council (582 B.C.), made up of representatives of twelve Greek peoples which administered the shrine and the Pythian Games, the cult of Apollo was well established and its influence on religion, politics, art, and commerce, through the famous oracle, was felt far beyond the borders of Greece.

After eight centuries of war, political strife, and the decline of religious influence, Theodosius II outlawed paganism in A.D. 426, seized the treasures, and carted most of them off to Constantinople. The shrine, like so many others a victim of the advent of Christianity, became a quarry for local builders.

In 1892, French archeologists moved the entire town of Delphi, which had grown up over the remnants of the once-famous shrine, to another spot nearby, and the excavations which followed have revealed to modern eyes much of its past glory.

At the top of the "sacred way," which was bordered with gifts and treasuries donated by the various Greek city-states and by victors in the games, stood the dominating structure of the sacred shrine, the colossal temple of the Pythian Apollo. Earthquakes and systematic destruction by the Christians have left only a few columns standing. The present temple, preceded by two earlier, more primitive structures, was built between 369 and 329 B.C. Xenodorous and Agathon were the architects, and the structure was financed by tribute exacted from the people of Phokis at the end of the Third Religious War. Before the temple was a large altar, gift of the island of Xios, in gratitude for their deliverance from the Persians, 494–479 B.C. Inside the temple, in the most sacred area in all Delphi, was a tripod over a cleft in the rock, from which issued the narcotic vapors which sent the Pythoness into her prophetic trance.

On a terrace below the shrine of Apollo is located the Marmaria, the precinct sacred to Athena Pronea. Here her temples, containing the earliest-known Doric elements, her treasuries, and altars stood amid a profusion of olive trees.

The Tholos, a round building on the Marmarian Terrace, whose specific use is still unknown, was the first round building with columns inside (Doric) and out (Corinthian). The latter, after Bassai's famous single column, are the oldest known use of Corinthian columns. The architect was Theodorus of Phocaea.

Between the shrine of Apollo and the Marmarian Terrace lie the remains of a gymnasium, scene of the training area for athletes participating in the Pythian Games, held in the stadium above. It contains a gallery, a racetrack, a wrestling ring, and a circular bathing-pool.

Amfissa ●

Parnassos

＊ ● DELPHI

ITEA ●

Naupaktos ●

● Patras

Gulf of Corinth

THEBES ●

DELPHI

● Corinth

AEGINA– TEMPLE OF APHAIA

ᒋᒋᒋᒋᒋᒋᒋᒋᒋᒋ

OVERLOOKING THE SARONIC GULF stands one of the largest and
most attractive of the Argo-Saronic islands, Aegina, known
in ancient times, because of military, political, and commercial rivalry, as the "eyesore of Athens." The two rival powers
cooperated against the Persian invasion, but once that common danger was over their enmity broke out anew and lasted
until the eventual triumph of Athens in 431 B.C. The Aegine-
tans were slaughtered, and the entire region appears to have
been deserted and its famous temple abandoned.

About eight miles north of the town of Aegina, on a wooded
hill above the Bay of Marina, is situated the Temple of A-
phaia. It was long thought by archeologists to be dedicated to
the goddess Athena, a belief substantiated by the discovery of
the statuary, in Parian marble, from the gables, in which the
central figure is that of Athena celebrating the victory of the
Greeks over the Trojans. In 1901, however, Feurtwangler, con-
ducting further excavations within the sanctuary, discovered
a broken slab from the 6th century B.C., the inscription on
which indicated that at the time the foundations were laid
down the temple had been dedicated to the local goddess,
Aphaia.

Aphaia, legend tells us, was born in Crete, where she was
called Brytomartis (Artemis), and was the daughter of Zeus
and Courmy. She was, according to Pindar, the patron of the
Island of Aegina.

On a beautiful mountain site, surrounded by pine woods,
stands the temple, built with the Aeginetan share of the spoils

from the Persian Wars. Its restoration, by Charles Garnier, is simple and tasteful, its only rivals being the Haephestion in Athens and the temple of Bassai in the Peloponnesus. Its fine sculptures, excavated in 1811, were bought by a prince of Bavaria in 1812, and are now housed in the Glyptothec in Munich. Of local limestone, a coating of stucco hiding the roughness of the stone, the remains indicate that the temple had upper galleries, reached by wooden stairs. The pediments and the roof were of Pentellic marble. No metopes having been found, it is presumed that they were originally of painted wood.

SARONIC GULF

AEGINA

TEMPLE OF APHAIA

AEGINA

CAPE PYRGOS

LINDOS, RHODES

LINDOS, WITH TWO HARBORS, was the largest maritime center of the three Dorian cities on the Island of Rhodes. On a headland, 375 feet above the sea, with one of the two harbors on either side, stands the Acropolis of the ancient town. As the site of the cult of Athena, it was one of the most venerated religious centers of the Dodecanese area. Legend has it that Danaüs and his fifty daughters landed here, after fleeing from Egypt, and erected the first sanctuary of Athena in gratitude for her help in their escape. It is known from the excavations that a number of temples had been built on this spot, from the 10th century onward.

The present temple to Lindia Athena was rebuilt in the 4th century B.C., and seems to have been constructed on the same plan as the small temple of Athena Nike, on the Acropolis in Athens. An immense statue of Athena, wearing a gold helmet and carrying a golden spear, once guarded the entrance to the temple. On the walls, Pindar's hymn in honor of Diagoras was engraved in letters of gold. Once the temple was surrounded by statuary and votive offerings; today there are remains of their engraved stone pediments, with the stains of rust indicating that metal clamps were once used to hold them firmly in place.

The most fascinating and imposing element of the sanctuary is its approach. Consisting of a colossal stairway with a double colonnade, its sweep and majesty make it one of the most impressive remains on the Island of Rhodes.

In the Middle Ages at the time of the Crusades, the Knights of Saint John of Jerusalem, fleeing from the invading Turks, settled for a time in Rhodes. Seeking a stronghold from which they might repell the Turks, they fortified the Acropolis and built a castle around it. To construct it, they employed much of the marble and the statuary which had stood in Athena's sanctuary. Traces of these remains can still be seen in the modern approach to the Acropolis, which lies through the ruins of the Knight's castle. This sacrilege, says the local legend, is why, after a long siege by the Turks, the Knights withdrew from the Island of Rhodes westward to Malta.

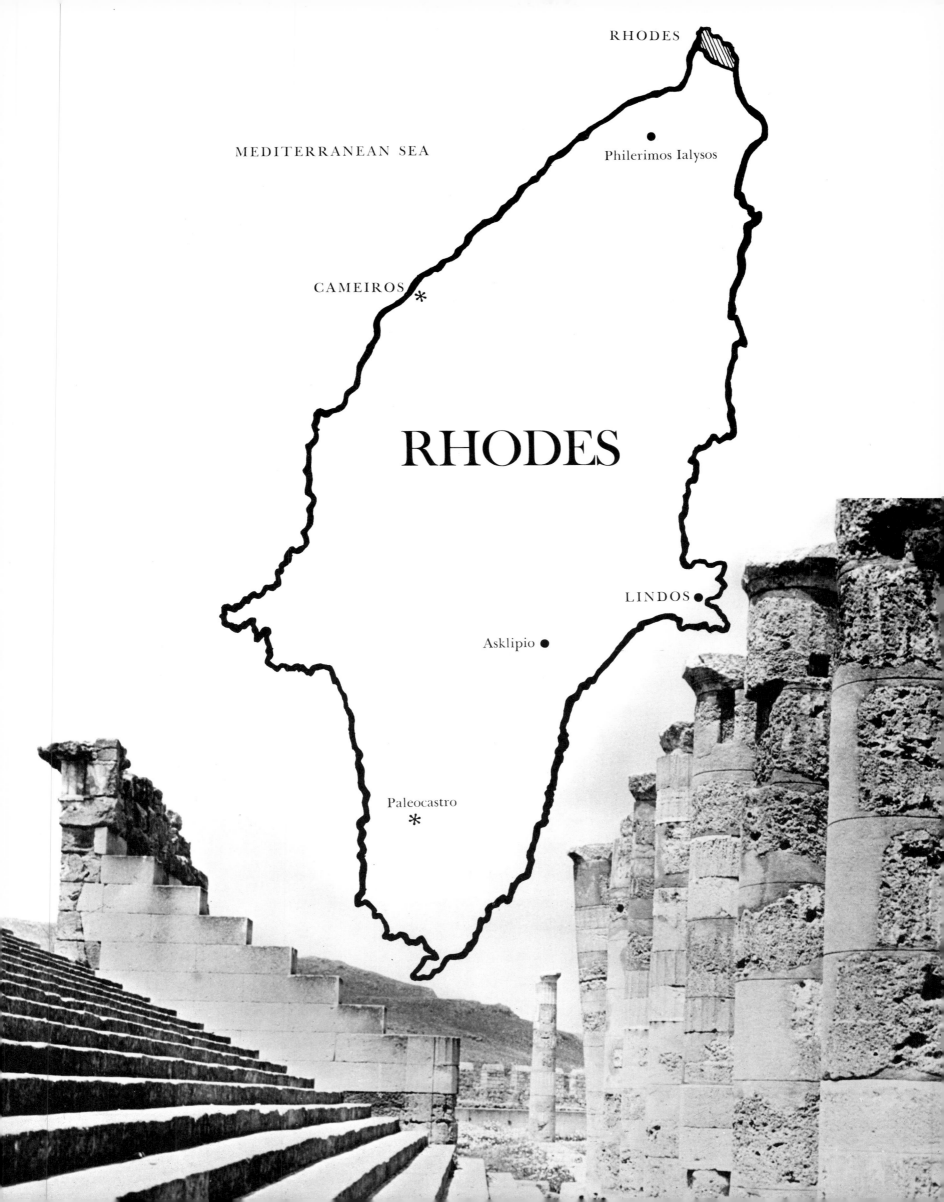

RHODES

MEDITERRANEAN SEA

RHODES

Philerimos Ialysos

CAMEIROS *

LINDOS ●

Asklipio ●

Paleocastro
*

DELOS

SOUTHEAST OF MYKONOS, IN THE HEART OF THE CYCLADES, lies small, rocky, uninhabited Delos. Here according to Homer's "Hymn to the Delian Apollo" Leto (Latonia), being with child by Zeus and refused refuge by all other lands (through fear of the wrath of Hera, Zeus's lawful wife), gave birth to Apollo and his sister Artemis, under a palm tree. Before this time, according to legend, Delos had been a floating island, but in honor of the birth of the god it was, henceforth, firmly anchored to the floor of the sea by pillars of diamond.

By the 7th century B.C., under the protection of the Island of Naxos, Delos had become the center of the Delian Amphictyonic Council, a loose political coalition of islands and their colonies, and the center and shrine of the cult of Delian Apollo. In 490 B.C. it was spared by the Persian invaders out of respect for the god Apollo; it later became the headquarters for the first Maritime League (477 B.C.), under the protection of Athens.

In 456 B.C., to secure the favor of Apollo, and just incidentally to gain control of the shrine's treasury, the Athenians purged and resanctified the island, and prohibited either birth or death to profane the island. From that day to the present, any inhabitant about to experience either was hastily removed to a neighboring island, and the sacred precinct remained undefiled. Around 315 B.C., Athens forsook Delos, which blossomed under independence. After the death of Alexander the Great, the island once again flourished and became an important commercial and shipping center, and, at one time, was the largest slave-market in the eastern Mediterranean.

Under the Romans the island was returned to the rule of the Athenians, and Delos prospered as never before. By the 2nd century A.D., however, having been sacked and destroyed twice by the Persian forces of Mithridates, according to Paussanius, the island had declined to the point where its only occupants were a few guardians of Apollo's shrine. From then until the the mid-19th century, the grandeurs of Delos served as a marble quarry for the Venetians, the Turks, the neighboring islands of Mykonos and Tinos, and pirates of various nationalities.

Among the many glories of the ancient shrine, excavated by the French School of Athens, beginning in 1873, was the so-called Terrace of Lions (lacking any indication of manes, it would seem more likely that it would have been a Terrace of Lionesses), guardians of the sacred shrine. Chiseled from Naxian marble, they were the magnificient gift of the citizens of Naxos in the 7th century B.C. At least nine "lions" once existed. Five were in place when discovered, and one sits, today, outside of the Arsenal in Venice. The only trace of the others is the base on which they once sat keeping watch over the sacred lake.

In the Sanctuary of the Alien Gods (for Apollo shared his shrine with his relatives and friends) stands the temple of the most widely worshipped Egyptian goddess, Isis, who, in her own country ruled heaven, earth and sea, as well as the underworld.

Cape Morou

Stadium

LOWER CITY

Sacred Lake

Cape Sykia

PORT

Sanctuary of Apollo

UPPER
CITY

Sanctuary of
Foreign Gods

RHENEIA

Theatre

MT. CYNTHUS
✳

DELOS

Quarries

Phourni Bay

ATHENS–
THE
PARTHENON

Eleusis

Sacred way to Eleusis

LYKABETTIS

ACROPOLIS   HEPHAESTEON

PIRAEUS

OLYMPIAN
ZEUS

Phaleron

Kalamaki

HYMETUS

ATHENS

Glyfada

STANDING ATOP THE ATHENIAN ACROPOLIS, the Parthenon represents, without doubt, the acme of Greek architectural achievement. At least two other temples, dedicated to Pallas Athena, had stood on the Acropolis before the present one was begun. The first, of porous stone, was started under Cleisthenes. Only the base had been laid when the First Persian War brought construction to a halt. After Marathon, work was resumed, this time in marble. The ground plan seems to have been the same as that of the present temple. Unfortunately, the resumption of the war with the Persians brought that effort, too, to an end. When the Persians drove the Athenians from their city, they occupied the Acropolis and razed the temple and the other sanctuaries to the ground. After the Persians were finally defeated, the Athenians extended their city walls to the Piraeus, and the remains of the second temple were employed in their construction.

In 454 B.C. Pericles had the treasures of Apollo's sanctuary at Delos removed to Athens for "safe keeping," and with these funds, seven years later, employed Ictinus, who had designed the temple of Apollo at Bassai, assisted by Callicrates and Phideas, to design Athena's new temple of Pentellic marble. The entire structure was completed between 447 and 438 B.C., although work on the pedimental sculptures by Phideas continued until 432 B.C. It was dedicated at the Panathenaic Festival of 438 B.C.—the "work of a single generation guided by a single inspiration."

Descriptions of the temple are found in guidebooks, architectural treatises, poems, prose, even mathematics, and any of these can give you the bare physical outlines. But to see it is to know that it defies verbal description. There is not a straight line in its structure: the columns are tilted, they are graduated in thickness as they approach the sky, their alignment is curved, the floor itself is not level. Every inch of the Parthenon compensates for the distortions built into the human eye, the end result being a visual masterpiece.

The colossal ivory and gold statue of Athena, by Phideas, was one of the "wonders" of the world. The gold with which she was adorned was made removable, in order that it might be removed and hidden, in case of invasion. There is a tale that, having been accused of stealing some of the gold for his own purposes, Phideas had it all removed and weighed, proving that the same weight of gold which he had been given to bedeck the statue was still there. The reflection of the sun from Athena's helmet and spear of gold could be seen by returning mariners from as far away as Cape Sounion. Paussanius tells us that at its foot was a basin of water, designed to maintain the humidity necessary to prevent the ivory from deteriorating.

Behind the shrine was a room where the statue of the goddess was decorated by Athenian maidens for the Panathenaic Festival. It was known in ancient times as the Parthenon or "room of the virgin." By the 4th century, this term was commonly applied to the entire temple, and thus it is known to us today.

For 2100 years this architectural jewel remained almost intact. Among the earliest known pictures of it was a sketch by the Bishop of Ancona. Entitled "Temple of Pallas," it shows the building when it was being used by Christians as the Catholic Church of Ste. Marie of Athens, in the 13th century.

On September 26, 1897, however, the Venetian forces on Philopappos Hill lobbed a shell into the powder magazine which the Turks had installed in the center of the Parthenon, destroying most of the interior and twenty-one exterior columns. Once the Turks had been ousted, Morosini, commander of the Venetian forces, attempted to remove a section of the West pediment, which he wished to take to Venice as a trophy. The tackle broke and the entire piece, including a figure of Poseidon and his horses, was destroyed. Lord Elgin of England, having received permission to remove a few blocks of stone and some small statuary, removed 247 feet of the frieze, fifteen metopes, and numerous statues, most of which are in the British Museum today.

Despite these ravages, the Parthenon is, today, one of the most exciting visual treats in all of the world. Plutarch has said "... though built in a short time, they [the temples on the Acropolis] have lasted for a long time. It is as if some flowing life and unaging spirit had been infused into the creation of these works."

The Porch of the Maidens on the Erecthium was a part of the rebuilding of the Acropolis, planned and encouraged by Pericles. Begun in 437 B.C., it was the work of the architect Mnesicles. The beginning of the Peloponnesian Wars in 432 B.C. prevented the completion of the project, but the porch with the Caryatides, who were probably sculpted by Callimachus, was finished. Except for the third maiden from the right, who is a substitute for the one which Lord Elgin spirited off to the British Museum, the porch, it is believed, remains as it was in the days of Classical Greece. The Erectheum, incidentally, was used as a Turkish harem in 1463.

ATHENS—
OLYMPIAN
ZEUS

BEYOND THE ARCH OF THE ROMAN EMPEROR HADRIAN, southeast of the Acropolis, stand the remains of the largest temple ever constructed in ancient Greece—that of Olympian Zeus. Although many altars to the father of all the gods existed in Classical Athens, no temple to him had ever been completed until after the birth of Christ.

In the late 6th century B.C., the tyrant Pisistratus created a plan for a temple to Zeus, on the Ionic order, of limestone, but the work had only proceeded as far as the foundations when Pisistratus died. Due to the people's refusal to complete anything begun by the tyrant, and due to the outbreak of the Persian Wars, this temple was never completed.

In the 2nd century B.C., the Syrian King Antiochus IV started over completely, with plans for a temple of the Corinthian order in marble. His death brought the project to a halt, for the second straight time. It is said, however, that the Roman General Sylla carried off a few of the Corinthian capitals to Rome, where they were used to decorate the Capitol and accounted for the the adoption of the Corinthian column as the signature of Roman architecture.

In A.D. 131–132 Hadrian, whose statue was finally to stand next to the gold and ivory Zeus within the temple, constructed or completed the temple. Just how much of Antiochus's effort remained at that time is unknown. (Hadrian also built Athen's first water system, which is still in use, and, until 1930, was the city's only source of running water!)

The temple in the Corinthian order, never used by the Greeks except in the interiors of their temples, is of marble, and originally contained 104 columns.

The Roman, Livy, said of the temple that it was "the only one in the world which has been conceived on a plan proportionate to the majesty of the god."

Over the centuries, in the course of successive invasions, the temple was almost completely destroyed. The site was used as a quarry for hundreds of years and as late as 1780 some of the columns were broken up, made into lime, and used in the construction of a Turkish mosque. Of the veritable forest of columns which once made up the temple, sixteen remain, one of which lies on the ground like the backbone of some prehistoric dinosaur.

ATHENS–
HEPHAESTEON

BELOW THE ACROPOLIS, on a small rise west of the Agora, near what is, even today, the quarter of the blacksmiths and metal-workers is situated one of the most intact of all Greek temples, the Hephaesteon. Dedicated to Hephaestos and shared by him with the goddess Athena, who enabled his followers to turn their work into things of beauty, the temple seems to be older than the Parthenon. Each of the two Olympians had a statue within the temple, and there was a joint festival each year, celebrating the invention of bronze-working by Hephaestos.

The sculptures on the frieze of the temple depict the exploits of Theseus, and for many years it was the popular belief that this was the temple of Theseus, the Thesion. More recent research has revealed that the temple was that of the God of the Forge, his cult having reached Athens by 600 B.C.

Of Pentellic marble and basically Doric in architecture, the temple, with a few exceptions, has remained more or less intact to the present day. Transformed into the Christian Church of Saint George during the 5th century A.D., except for interior changes the temple suffered no major damage. During the Turkish occupation, the temple was outside the confines of the shrunken city of Athens, and again escaped destruction at the hands of an invader. An earthquake in 1807 and a severe lightning storm in 1821 damaged several columns slightly, but, as of today, it remains practically unchanged since the days of Pericles.

One singular feature of the temple is that it seems to have

been surrounded, as it is today, by a formal garden, of sorts (an unusual practice for the Greeks). In the rocks around the temple, there are cuttings which seem to have been intended to hold earthenware flowerpots or trees—one of the earliest signs of landscape gardening in connection with a temple.